POCKET
COCO CHANEL
WISDOM

**Witty quotes and wise words
from a fashion icon**

Pocket Coco Chanel Wisdom

First published in 2017 by Hardie Grant Books, an imprint of Hardie Grant Publishing

Hardie Grant Books (UK)
52-54 Southwark Street
London SE1 1UN

Hardie Grant Books (Australia)
Ground Floor, Building 1
658 Church Street
Melbourne, VIC 3121

hardiegrantbooks.com

Cover illustration © Michele Rosenthal 2017
Internal illustrations © Daisy Dudley 2017

British Library Cataloguing-in-Publication Data. A catalogue record
for this book is available from the British Library.

ISBN: 978-1-78488-139-9

Publisher: Kate Pollard
Senior Editor: Kajal Mistry
Editorial Assistant: Hannah Roberts
Publishing Assistant: Eila Purvis
Design: Daisy Dudley
Cover Illustration: Michele Rosenthal
Colour Reproduction by p2d

Printed and bound in China by 1010

POCKET
COCO CHANEL
WISDOM

Witty quotes and wise words
from a fashion icon

hardie grant books

CONTENTS

Coco Chanel on...

"

A WOMAN WHO CUTS HER HAIR IS ABOUT TO CHANGE HER LIFE.

"

"

FASHION SHOULD
BE DISCUSSED
ENTHUSIASTICALLY,
AND SANELY; AND ABOVE
ALL WITHOUT POETRY,
WITHOUT LITERATURE.

"

"

FASHION FADES; ONLY STYLE REMAINS THE SAME.

"

"

FASHION SHOULD DIE AND DIE QUICKLY, IN ORDER THAT COMMERCE MAY SURVIVE.

"

"

THE MOMENT I HAD TO
CHOOSE BETWEEN THE MAN
I LOVED AND MY DRESSES,
I CHOSE MY DRESSES.

"

"

A FASHION THAT DOES
NOT REACH THE STREETS
IS NOT A FASHION.

"

> "
>
> COUTURE IS NOT THEATRE,
> AND FASHION IS NOT AN ART,
> IT IS A CRAFT.
>
> "

"

SIMPLICITY IS THE
KEYNOTE OF ALL TRUE
ELEGANCE.

"

66

FASHION IS ARCHITECTURE: IT IS A MATTER OF PROPORTIONS.

99

"

A WOMAN CAN BE OVERDRESSED BUT NEVER OVER ELEGANT.

"

66

A BEAUTIFUL DRESS MAY
LOOK BEAUTIFUL ON
A HANGER, BUT THAT MEANS
NOTHING. IT MUST BE SEEN
ON THE SHOULDERS, WITH
THE MOVEMENT OF
THE ARMS, THE LEGS,
AND THE WAIST.

99

66

FASHION IS NOT AN ART, IT IS A JOB.

99

"

FASHION HAS TWO
PURPOSES: COMFORT AND
LOVE. BEAUTY COMES
WHEN FASHION SUCCEEDS.

"

"

FASHION IS NOT SOMETHING
THAT EXISTS IN DRESSES
ONLY. FASHION IS IN THE
SKY, IN THE STREET,
FASHION HAS TO DO WITH
IDEAS, THE WAY WE LIVE,
WHAT IS HAPPENING.

"

"

MOST WOMEN DRESS FOR
MEN AND WANT TO BE
ADMIRED. BUT THEY
MUST ALSO BE ABLE TO
MOVE, TO GET INTO A CAR
WITHOUT BURSTING
THEIR SEAMS.

"

66

FASHION CHANGES, BUT STYLE ENDURES.

99

"

BEFORE YOU LEAVE THE HOUSE, LOOK IN THE MIRROR AND REMOVE ONE ACCESSORY.

"

"

A DRESS IS NEITHER
A TRAGEDY, NOR A PAINTING;
IT IS A CHARMING AND
EPHEMERAL CREATION,
NOT AN EVERLASTING
WORK OF ART.

"

"

A FINE FABRIC IS BEAUTIFUL
IN ITSELF, BUT THE MORE
LAVISH A DRESS IS, THE
POORER IT BECOMES.

"

"

ONE SHOULDN'T SPEND ALL
ONE'S TIME DRESSING.
ALL ONE NEEDS ARE TWO
OR THREE SUITS, AS LONG
AS THEY AND EVERYTHING
TO GO WITH THEM
ARE PERFECT.

"

66

LUXURY MUST BE COMFORTABLE, OTHERWISE IT IS NOT LUXURY.

99

"

FASHION HAS BECOME
A JOKE. THE DESIGNERS
HAVE FORGOTTEN THAT
THERE ARE WOMEN
INSIDE THE DRESSES.

"

"

PERFUME IS THE UNSEEN,
UNFORGETTABLE, ULTIMATE
ACCESSORY OF FASHION...
[IT] HERALDS YOUR
ARRIVAL AND PROLONGS
YOUR DEPARTURE.

"

"

THE BEST COLOUR IN THE
WHOLE WORLD IS THE ONE
THAT LOOKS GOOD ON YOU.

"

66

ELEGANCE IS REFUSAL.

99

"

ADORNMENT, WHAT A
SCIENCE! BEAUTY, WHAT
A WEAPON! MODESTY,
WHAT ELEGANCE!

"

> **"**
>
> COSTUME JEWELLERY IS
> NOT MADE TO GIVE WOMEN
> AN AURA OF WEALTH, BUT
> TO MAKE THEM BEAUTIFUL.
>
> **"**

"

ELEGANCE IS NOT THE
PREROGATIVE OF THOSE
WHO HAVE JUST ESCAPED
FROM ADOLESCENCE,
BUT OF THOSE WHO HAVE
ALREADY TAKEN POSSESSION
OF THEIR FUTURE.

"

"

IT'S ALWAYS BETTER TO BE SLIGHTLY UNDERDRESSED.

"

66

I AM AGAINST FASHION
THAT DOESN'T LAST.

99

Coco Chanel on...

66

A WOMAN HAS THE AGE
SHE DESERVES.

99

66

LOOK FOR THE WOMAN
IN THE DRESS. IF THERE
IS NO WOMAN,
THERE IS NO DRESS.

99

"

A GIRL SHOULD BE
TWO THINGS:
CLASSY AND FABULOUS.

"

66

A WOMAN EQUALS ENVY
PLUS VANITY PLUS CHATTER
PLUS A CONFUSED MIND.

99

"

I DON'T UNDERSTAND HOW
A WOMAN CAN LEAVE THE
HOUSE WITHOUT MAKING
HERSELF UP A LITTLE...

"

66

WOMEN OUGHT TO PLAY THEIR WEAKNESS, NEVER THEIR STRENGTH.

99

66

A WOMAN WHO DOESN'T WEAR PERFUME HAS NO FUTURE.

99

"

SOLITUDE MAY HELP A MAN
TOWARDS ACHIEVEMENT
BUT IT DESTROYS A WOMAN.

"

"

A GIRL SHOULD BE TWO THINGS: WHO AND WHAT SHE WANTS.

"

“

A WOMAN WITH GOOD SHOES
IS NEVER UGLY.

”

Coco Chanel on...

"

PRIDE IS PRESENT IN
WHATEVER I DO. IT IS THE
SECRET OF MY STRENGTH...
IT IS BOTH MY FLAW AND
MY VIRTUE.

"

"

SOME PEOPLE THINK
LUXURY IS THE OPPOSITE
OF POVERTY. IT IS NOT.
IT IS THE OPPOSITE
OF VULGARITY.

"

> ❝
>
> # EXTRAVAGANT THINGS DIDN'T SUIT ME.
>
> ❞

> **"**
>
> ## ONE CANNOT BE FOREVER INNOVATING. I WANT TO CREATE CLASSICS.
>
> **"**

"

I CANNOT TAKE ORDERS FROM ANYONE ELSE, EXCEPT IN LOVE.

"

"

MAY MY LEGEND GAIN
GROUND – I WISH IT A LONG
AND HAPPY LIFE.

"

"

I... AM AN ODIOUS PERSON.

"

"

I WAS THE ONE WHO
CHANGED, IT WASN'T
FASHION. I WAS THE ONE
WHO WAS IN FASHION.

"

"

I AM AN ARTISAN, SO I WANT
A PERFUME THAT IS
COMPOSED – A PARADOX.

"

> ❝
>
> MY LIFE HAS BEEN
> MERELY A PROLONGED
> CHILDHOOD.
>
> ❞

"

ARROGANCE IS IN EVERYTHING I DO.

"

"

BUT I LIKED WORK. I HAVE
SACRIFICED EVERYTHING
TO IT, EVEN LOVE. WORK HAS
CONSUMED MY LIFE.

"

66

I DON'T CARE WHAT
YOU THINK ABOUT ME.
I DON'T THINK
ABOUT YOU AT ALL.

"

THERE ARE A LOT OF
DUCHESSES, BUT THERE
CAN ONLY BE ONE
COCO CHANEL.

"

"

I AM NOT A HEROINE.
BUT I HAVE CHOSEN
THE PERSON I WANTED
TO BE.

"

"

THE CHILD THAT I WAS IS WITH ME TODAY.

"

Coco Chanel on...

"

THE MOST COURAGEOUS ACT IS STILL TO THINK FOR YOURSELF. ALOUD.

"

"

THE BEST THINGS IN LIFE
ARE FREE. THE SECOND
BEST THINGS ARE VERY,
VERY EXPENSIVE.

"

66

J'AIME LA VIE!
I FEEL THAT TO LIVE IS A
WONDERFUL THING.

99

66

MY LIFE DIDN'T PLEASE ME, SO I CREATED MY LIFE.

99

"

THERE IS A TIME FOR WORK,
AND A TIME FOR LOVE. THAT
LEAVES NO OTHER TIME.

"

"

ONLY THOSE WITH NO
MEMORY INSIST ON THEIR
ORIGINALITY.

"

"

NOBODY CAN LIVE WITH LOW HORIZONS.

"

"

SINCE EVERYTHING IS IN
OUR HEADS, WE HAD
BETTER NOT LOSE THEM.

"

66

NATURE GIVES YOU THE FACE
YOU HAVE AT TWENTY; IT
IS UP TO YOU TO MERIT THE
FACE YOU HAVE AT FIFTY.

99

66

AGEING IS A STATE OF
MIND. ONE MUST
KEEP ENTHUSIASM
AND CURIOSITY.

99

"

FOR ANY HUMAN BEING WHO
THINKS OF HIMSELF OR
HERSELF IS ALREADY DEAD.

"

"

THERE IS NO TIME FOR
CUT-AND-DRIED MONOTONY.

"

66

YOU LIVE BUT ONCE; YOU
MIGHT AS WELL BE AMUSING.

99

66

YOU CAN BE GORGEOUS AT
THIRTY, CHARMING AT
FORTY, AND IRRESISTIBLE
FOR THE REST OF YOUR LIFE.

99

"

LIFE IS A SOLEMN AFFAIR, SINCE IT CAUSED MOTHERS TO CRY.

"

66

HOW MANY CARES ONE
LOSES WHEN ONE DECIDES
NOT TO BE SOMETHING
BUT TO BE SOMEONE.

99

Coco Chanel on...

Succe

66

TO PLEASE IS TO BE
SOMEONE WHO LISTENS,
WHO SEEMS
SOMEWHAT FRAGILE.

99

66

IN 1919, I WOKE UP FAMOUS.

99

"

TO ACHIEVE GREAT THINGS, WE MUST FIRST DREAM.

"

"

IN ORDER TO BE
IRREPLACEABLE ONE MUST
ALWAYS BE DIFFERENT.

"

"

SUCCESS IS MOST OFTEN
ACHIEVED BY THOSE WHO
DON'T KNOW THAT FAILURE
IS INEVITABLE.

"

66

THOSE WHO CREATE ARE
RARE; THOSE WHO CANNOT
ARE NUMEROUS.
THEREFORE, THE LATTER
ARE STRONGER.

99

"

THOSE ON WHOM LEGENDS ARE BUILT ARE THEIR LEGENDS.

"

"

GENTLENESS DOESN'T
GET WORK DONE, UNLESS
YOU HAPPEN TO BE
A HEN LAYING EGGS.

"

SOURCES

Baxter-Wright, Emma (2012) *The Little Book of Chanel*, Carlton Books – pp. **19, 41**

Chaney, Lisa (2011) *Chanel: An Intimate Life*, Fig Tree – pp. **37, 52, 63**

Cosgrave, Bronwyn (2012) *Vogue on Coco Chanel*, Quadrille Publishing – pp. **12, 14, 16, 17, 20, 22, 29, 30, 33, 34, 35, 40, 44, 60, 79**

Haedrich, Marcel (1972) *Coco Chanel: Her Life, Her Secrets*, Little, Brown – p. **91**

Harper's Bazaar, 6th February 2014 – p. **24**

Harper's Bazaar, 11th November 2016 – pp. **8, 15, 17, 46, 48, 78**

Hess, Megan (2015) *Coco Chanel: The Illustrated World of a Fashion Icon*, Hardie Grant Books – pp. **10, 28, 31, 36, 49, 65, 90**

International Business Times, 18th August 2015 – pp. **21, 32**

Karbo, Karen (2009) *The Gospel According to Coco Chanel: Life Lessons from the World's Most Elegant Woman*, Rowan & Littlefield – pp. **27, 42, 53, 70, 85**

Kirov, Blago (2014) *The Famous: Book 3*, CreateSpace Independent Publishing Platform – pp. **71, 74, 75, 93**

Madsen, Axel (2015) *Chanel: A Woman of Her Own*, Open Road Media – pp. **62, 76**

Marie Claire, 23rd July 2014 – pp. **72, 77**

Marie Claire, 4th October 2016 – pp. **23, 64, 73, 81**

Matchbook Magazine, 29th April 2013 – pp. **55, 82, 45**

Morand, Paul (2013) *The Allure of Chanel*, Pushkin Press – pp. **26, 57, 61, 66, 80, 84**

New York Review of Books, 9th October 2014 – pp. **43, 58**

Simon, Linda (2011) *Coco Chanel*, Reaktion Books – pp. **45, 47, 56, 67, 88, 89**

Telegraph, 5th September 2010 – p. **94**

Telegraph, 1st October 2010 – p. **54**

Vogue, 2nd October 2013 – pp. **9, 11, 25**

Women Who Wear, 27th November 2015 – pp. **13, 59, 83, 92**